IN THE ORCHARD

IN THE ORCHARD

Poetry by
CHARLES W. PRATT

Drawings by
Arthur Balderacchi

THE TIDAL PRESS

1986

ACKNOWLEDGEMENTS

The Atlantic Monthly: Relativity
The Christian Science Monitor: The Secret of Maple Country
Commonweal: Balloon Flight; Brass Rubbing; Evening Meditation
    in a Cathedral Town; Fibonacci Sequence; On the Beauty of the
    Universal Order; Raking Leaves in New England
Harvard Magazine: Stones
The Hiram Poetry Review: The Poet Attempts to Console His Wife,
    Who Has Just Put His Wallet through the Washing Machine;
    Thirty-five
Light Year '86: A Fable in Two Languages
The Literary Review: The Bliss of Bears; Two Poets in Vermont; The
    Quiet of the Country
The Lyric: Vermont House
Mazagine: The Infestation
Poetry: Tracks
Poetry Northwest: Winter Squash
Soundings East: For Sarah

"Relativity" also appeared in the 1984 *Anthology of Magazine Verse
and Yearbook of American Poetry.*

Poems copyright 1985 by Charles W. Pratt
Drawings copyright 1985 by Arthur Balderacchi

Library of Congress Catalog Card Number: LCC85-51420
ISBN: P B-0-930954-27-0
SECOND PRINTING

THE TIDAL PRESS
Cranberry Isles, Maine 04625

for my family—and others
who have encouraged

Heating with Wood

Tonight, stovewood
Won't light. Paper,
Sticks flare, die. Char,
Cold smoke. Huddle over
Dead iron, try, fail,
Try, till at last
Wood dried by false starts
Nurtures reluctant flame.
Yes, there's an easier way:
The oil burner's click
And acquiescent sigh.

AUTHOR'S NOTE

I recently read in a dentist's waiting room a magazine article which explained that paying quiet, careful attention to something outside of oneself is good for the blood pressure. The act of writing is to me a way of paying such attention, and thereby of bringing self and outside world into harmony. To the extent that I've succeeded, perhaps the reader will experience a similar sense of harmony, and enjoy a similar improvement of the blood pressure.

The poems beginning with "In the Woods" and ending with "The Gift" form a sort of unit. In June, 1984, my family and I moved to a small apple orchard and I took a half year's leave of absence from my teaching to work the orchard and to complete this sequence of poems. The project was supported jointly by a grant from The New Hampshire Commission on the Arts and The National Endowment for the Arts, support for which I was and am extremely grateful.

The project was supported jointly by a grant from The New Hampshire Commission on the Arts and The National Endowment for the Arts.

✗✗✗✗✗

CONTENTS

RELATIVITY

GREED AND GRACE IN THE ORCHARD

In the Woods

What's he doing, you'd wonder, here in the very
Middle of the woods, shouldering logs from a stack
Someone cut and left so long ago
How could it promise any significant heat
Across two hundred branch-littered, bouldery
Yards to drop them onto a raggeder heap?
Forth and back, forth again and back
Over pine needles and crunchy patches of snow,
Log's weight pressing his feet into every
Irregularity of terrain, nose to the sweet
Heavy fungus smell of sodden bark, he keeps
Going. And when a log slips from his shoulder
At last, like guilt or a cherished injury,
For a moment he's almost light enough to fly.

Learning to Prune

> "I bless thee, Lord, because I grow
> Among the trees, which in a row
> To thee both fruit and order owe."
> *George Herbert, "Paradise"*

Jock perches in the top
of the apple like a wild
turkey (I've seen them here),
the sound of his saw
nastying a little the nice
March day: south slope, false spring.
I, on the ground,
circle my tree slowly,
reaching my long pole-clippers up
to the suckers and branches I want
out. My neck aches as I
jerk the handle and a branch
drops. It snags, I flip it clear.
I had it in mind this morning
I'd get a poem out of pruning,
about discipline, I thought, and form,
like Herbert's "Paradise" —
but Jock has taught me already
it's not a question of that so much
as of opening up the center
to sun and air, taking out what

grows too upright or crosses,
and keeping the top in reach.
He's down from the tree now, his clippers
snick quickly, he talks
to himself as he works.
Each time I finish a tree,
maybe one to three of his,
he comes over to check,
snips a little here and there,
and tells me I'm doing fine,
though I cut more than he would, probably,
on a Cortland, that is;
you can let a Cortland grow thicker; with Cortlands
people don't mind a little green on the apple,
but they like their Macs red.
Towards 5:00 — I'm tired, but
ready to go on as long as he can —
he says it's time to quit.
We go in and drink hot tea
with honey, talk a bit,
and then he's off, clipper pole
poking from the Volkswagen's open window.
A few more days like this with him,
he says, and I'll have the swing of it,
I'll be on my own.

Stones

Mowing the old field, he thinks mostly
Of stones, boulders really, knucklebones
Of buried giants, porpoises
Somersaulting through the surf of earth,
Playful as porpoises the way they break
His blades if he's careless. But that's *his*
Fancy, he knows; it's not they who play
With him but he with them, at least
Those he can see, shaving them close
And fast as he dares. Other times only
Memory or a tuft of higher grass
Reminds him where they are in time to
Swerve where granite bulges. So
Hawk's shadow crossing his shoulder, clouds'
Metamorphoses he ignores; stones
Keep his eyes low to study
The way the land lies, the grass grows.
They wait, they do nothing, they give
Only themselves, their one assertion:
Stone. And he is grateful for them,
Presences he can almost count on.

Answering the Questions

He looks up from his shingling and squints over
The valley where the hidden river runs.
"I wouldn't mind retiring here myself."
"Neither would I,"

I answer drily, but wonder whether I have
In giving up my paycheck to live off
Land and wife in a state of antisocial
Insecurity.

150 apple trees, three garden plots,
Dirt-crammed fingernails and a stiff back
Are my evidence that this is no pulling out
But a digging in,

No retreat but a strategic withdrawal
From territory too long occupied,
No longer friendly, not worth holding on to,
To advance on a new front.

The reporter shuts his notebook. Unconvinced?
Print this, I tell him, this is the one thing that matters:
Whatever the pressures, I have retracted nothing,
And will not retract.

He's gone back to hammering on the roof,
I go back to digging in the garden,
And the river goes on running through the valley,
Unobserved.

Spray or Pray

With apples, it's either
Spray or pray, I'm told, and feeling
Ill-at-ease with both, but being,
I guess, inevitably 20th century,
Choose to spray. 5:00 A.M.,
Before the wind rises to spread
Poison where it isn't wanted,
Dressed like an astronaut or lunatic
Religious in hooded
Waterproof, respirator, goggles,
I drive my tractor from tree to tree,
Dragging the tank of noxious stuff
I've reluctantly weighed and mixed.
I dismount, point the spraygun upwards,
And squeeze the trigger: a vague
Haze drifts over tree,
Grass, sprayer, tractor, me,
Fogs my goggles till I stumble
As though through some foreign element.

Hating the poison, hating the noisy
Sprayer engine which quits from time to time
Just to remind me who's in control,
Hating the sun which dazzles
And steams me in my waterproof,
Hating the wind, hating even
The apple trees and especially
My own incompetent self,
I half do what they say I must do,
And hope without faith that it will make
Some difference. (In fact,
The apples are scabby anyway,
But I've killed the worst pests,
Plum curculios and maggots.)
In what, then, *do* I have faith,
The way, at night, going from barn to house,
The body knows its way without misstep:
Assumes the invisible orchard?

Greed and Grace in the Orchard

The druid priestess, capitalist to the core,
Who sold the orchard to us didn't know,
Or didn't choose to tell,
That down in the hollow by the well
Among the chokecherry and juniper
Wild blueberries grow.

Whether she thought bushes inferior
Gods, or the berries too small and few
For profit, she consigned
Us gratis the pleasures of both find
And fruit. And when the tractor that she swore
Was good as new

Wheel-deep in daisies is dreaming like Ferdinand,
Some inner organ broken beyond my skill,
While maggot flies lay
Eggs in the apples I can't spray,
Or weeds in the garden have gotten the upper hand,
I go downhill

To the nets I've spread — just outcast from the commune
Of the wild — to keep the catbirds in their place,
And crouched in the stagnant air
Pick until every bush is bare
And berries fill my bowl with unearned income,
Nature's grace.

Mosquitoes seethe in the bottom. As I sweat and slap,
I imagine blueberry midnight. The moon is full,
And the priestess, naked, dances
Before her trees, which stretch out branches
Trembling with the bumper crop of apples
Fattening to fall.

The Quiet of the Country

∷

The baseboard cricket's at it again,
Playing and playing his one refrain,
As constant as a shrewish wife
Who's condemned herself to you for life,
At it, at it, at it again,
At it again and again until
You, too, are single-minded: kill
The baseboard cricket at it again,
At it, at it, at it again.

∷

All summer, one by one,
The apples drop. We shudder
At the impact in the bone

As if, far off, big guns
Echoed from war long over
Or war still to begin.

∷

Seen from this hilltop, stars
At eyelevel quiver in the night.
Looking through branches, you'd guess airplanes,
But watch a while and they still keep their place.

Right the first time, of course. They race
Burning through space, roaring like the dragstrip
Four miles away, where under crackling lights
Pickupsful chug beer and cheer the cars.

On the Beauty of the Universal Order

Odd
to think that God
designed
the apple tree
so perfectly
to catch on crooked branch, in acute crotch
the narrow pointed ladder Adam would invent
to ease his labors when as punishment
for apple-snatching, he was sent
forth wandering from the garden. Odd that I,
without design,
at least of mine,
now at the end of almost fifty years should find
myself here high
on springy rungs, the ladder like an arrow pointing me
towards dangling planets. I grasp a branch and lean
over the void to grip
the perfect apple at the branch's tip.

Brown
below my feet, turned earth tells where
this morning I clawed down
ladderless to find
and fumble up to air,
knobby and bare
as baby skulls, huge as pre-Edenic continents,
my Kennebecs:
earth-apples. One,
under my hand,
stirred, shook off a clod,
became bloat toad.
Also child of God.

Porcupine Sonnet

Picking up drops from under one of my apples,
I see by a farther tree I claim as mine
A small fur hat some passing Russian's left.
It moves. Black eyes, stub tail: the porcupine.

He surrounds an apple, mouths his way around it,
And waddles off to find a sixteenth course.
Although he'd like to, he doesn't eat enough
To force me into any display of force.

Two nations not at war and not at peace,
We treat each other with benign neglect,
Gnawing in silence, silently filling boxes —
A tolerant coexistence I suspect

Sooner or later I'll have somehow to pay for,
And make him pay for.

Harvest

The trees, I'm told, have stood here fifty years —
Bearers still. The motherly Cortlands, fat
As their dusky apples, cookers, firm in pies.
The Macs more upright, sparer, the apples —
This year, at least — scarcer, smaller, brighter,
Flecked with little lights. And the Wageners,
Bristling with apples from a thousand spurs,
The fruit a modest russet, turning as it ripens
To scarlet, apples from a Book of Hours.

Sweetness seethes from the press, foams
In the bucket; I turn with the handle
Under the mild October sun
That brings back summer, softened. Sunyellow
Hornets, now, mellowed from when,
In August, the mower brought their stinging
Hubbub up from underground,
Nuzzle my sticky fingers, gentle as cows,
Swoon to that foaming sweetness where they drown.

Midnight, midwinter. Under the full moon
The trees, like twisting smoke, like rocks
Whorled by tides of air,
Stand stock-still in their shadows
On the new snow, precise and mysterious
As spiders on a linen tablecloth.
Arrested, I look out, investing
Them with the patient merit
And deliberate innocence I would learn of them.

Interlude

The sun slips lower. Yesterday it snowed—
A frozen inch or two: enough. For now
Forget the maul and wedge, the unsplit wood,
All that you *should* for winter, grab the cracked sled
(Plastic) from the barn, run, leap . . . slide,
Belly flattened to the hard hill's hide—
Mad bronco bucking till the cowboy's spilled,
Mad lover answering hips with surging hips—
While orderly ranks of apples stand appalled,
Black-robed widows, blurring with your speed,
And westward the sunset, row on row, applauds
In frenzied violets, crimsons. Now the sled slows,
Stops. Bring in the wood. Tonight, deep cold.

Exercise of the Imagination

To go to sleep, he said, when you have insomnia,
Imagine a field of perfect white; and whenever
Anything appears in the field, erase it. And then erase the eraser.
I try to imagine it that way: the orchard as it is at this moment,
The particular light of this November afternoon, the way that
    the light
Now, at this instant, turns the small crinkled apple leaves orange,
    not bright
Orange, but warm, an orange that somehow insists
In the heart on the importance of this instant, of each particular
    instant,
And the clouds piling up to the east there, over the woods, and
    the slope of the falling
Of that leaf in the wind against the slope of the hill
Erased
As by deep December snow — so deep as to ungrass the slope,
    untree the woods, unbird the sky, unsky the universe, white,
    white, and then that white
Erased,
All consciousness of white erased by white . . .

And when you are asleep, black, black — not the sleep of dreams
But the sleep between dreams, the single snap of the fingers
That takes you through who knows what void, what space of
    time to morning . . .

And if there is no morning?

            The long disgrace
Of history erased . . .

            And all that we see,
All that our beautiful seeing makes beautiful.

[19]

The Gift

after a stained-glass window
by Gabriel Loire

In Gabriel's window, Eve offers the apple again,
And could Adam refuse
Her on her knees raising the apple bright
As heart's blood, as hearth-fire?
The fish approves, the donkey, the ram, the dove,
A shimmer of blues
Overhead; and the snake is winding around them the golden
Coils of desire.
Fear not — it is Gabriel's voice in the throats of the flowers:
The flesh is sweet.
Be joyful, fear not, for you are filled with the light.
Take the apple, and eat.

Raking Leaves in New England

Liberated, laid-off, have it either way,
These fallen leaves for me are only work.
I'd rather leave their brilliant litter lay
To pleasure grass and children, but my rake
Drags me responsibly across the lawn
As if it were the branch to which I cling
Against the wind that brings vain beauty down.
The dark pure men alone will stand till spring.

Winter Squash

In bare December, the spirit seeks out matter.
You turn from the window and go down to the cellar,
Past braids of onions hanging from the rafters,
Sacks of potatoes and carrots, boxes of apples,
To stroke the hard smooth skin of the winter squashes,
Tawny butternut and ribbed green acorn,
Row after row on shelves, like words in Webster's,
Waiting. You pick one up. Sun on your shoulder
Weighs as you stoop to plant, to weed, to water.
Cool and dark, you stand in the buried cellar
Forming your sentence, then climb back up to winter.

Tracks

Trailing an earlier skier through the pines,
I stop where he stopped, at a sudden stone:

SUSANNAH HOLMAN

wife of

JOSEPH BROWN

1785–1812

(Joseph Brown is carved as square and deep,
As if to say he has to bear more weight
Of years, pain, guilt to judgment); and then a footnote,
So low he's scraped the snow away to read

also an infant daughter

                           in italics, nameless.
We pause together, leaning on our poles.
Rest, Susannah Holman, from your hard delivery.
Rest, infant daughter. And wherever your grave may be,
Rest, Joseph Brown. The tracks lead smoothly on.

The Secret of Maple Country

Drill, at winter's
First hint of relaxing,
Holes in a ring
Every eight inches
Around the maples,
Beads on a string.
Tap.
Sap
Plinks into tins,
Plonks into plastic,
Splashes and spills
Till poured to a pan
And boiled over woodflame,
Forty clear gallons
Down to one with the pale
Gold shivering sweetness
Of sun on snow.
So
While the nights stay cold.
Spring
Clouds the issue.

The Bliss of Bears

for Cabot Lyford

A bear on a raspberry bender, Vermont friends say,
Lies on his back and squirms headfirst through the stalks
Like a bulldozer flattening trees for a porkbarrel highway,
Clawing the berries down into ravenous jaws.
He stains his fur coat blood-purple as he blunders backwards,
Nothing on earth but his gullet he gives a damn for —
Why should he worry? He'll be asleep all winter;
No freezer to fill, no neighbors to put up jam for.
He didn't set out this patch — didn't weed it or thin it,
Maybe manured it one day just passing by,
But gave it never a thought until he was in it,
Backstroking bearwise, gazing up at the sky,
Which dangles over his nose its ripe red riches
While earth underneath him curries his ticks and itches.

Two Poets in Vermont

When Robert Frost played ball with John Crowe Ransom,
He hit long flies, and Ransom, on narrow legs,
Chased them into the weeds beyond the field.
He took off his coat, his vest, his broad-brimmed hat,
Unbuttoned his shirt; and still the ball arched out,
Out, out beyond his reach. That's what we mean
When we say that Robert Frost was down-to-earth:
"Now, John, you go hunt in the weeds a while;
I'll stay right here. But whatever it is you find,
Baseball or snake, remember: I sent you in."

Vermont House

This house, half-way uphill,
Is crooked from roof to sill;
I climb a biased floor
To yank at a sticky door,
Or watch a child's ball roll
Down to a tilted wall,
Till I swear by the grin of the Devil
Nothing is on the level,
Nothing the eye can view
Establishes the true,
Though the whole thing hangs together
Solid enough to weather
Storms of the normal kind:
The emblem of my mind.

Afternoon Walk

A caterpillar on the road
Lies dead,
Pellucid fluid oozing from
Anus and head,
The busy legs, the crunching jaws
Now motionless.
Being no sort of naturalist
I cannot guess
From what green depredations he
Has been brought low
Or what highflying destiny
He must forego,
But so displayed against the tar,
Hairless, immense,
And unexplained, his corpse assumes
Significance.
Here lies an Everyman whose soul,
Liquid and clear,
Has day by wasted day leaked out
And year by year,
Till he transfixes with a black,
Accusing eye,
His alter ego on the road,
Just passing by.

RELATIVITY

Fibonacci Sequence

Stars,
as
we see
them at least,
refuse to keep their
distances, prefer company,
declare themselves chairs, bears, dippers, sweet milky highways.
So the hermit is sustained, isn't he, in dark privacy by the invisible
strings by which he dangles from the high hand of his God?
So many bees stinging night's flesh!
The passion of all
singleness
to keep
in
touch.

Relativity

for Lotte Jacobi

As we go down in the dark the slight
Icy slope to the car, the grip of your hands
On my shoulders tells me you're right

Behind me and upright. I don't understand
Relativity, but forty-some years ago
You photographed Albert Einstein, and

Today I saw his soft eyes, below
The fine accumulation of his hair,
Random, gentle, abstract hair, as though

His thought like pipesmoke issued on the air;
I saw his sailboat drifting, his violin
Waiting his hands. And always I felt you there,

About the age I am you must have been,
Holding your camera as if you took a friend
By the shoulders to show him something you'd seen.

If the universe is a slope all things descend,
If the speed of light is the only absolute,
What every atom dreams of as its end,

On this icy path, if I should slip, would we shoot
Like lasers into the dark, a double star?
Old hands on my shoulders, be my parachute,

Help me go slow. And so we reach the car,
Waiting to take us wherever we're headed tonight,
And laughing, say to each other, "Here we are!"

Driving to Cape Cod

Summers, when he drove us to Cape Cod,
My father missed red lights, abruptly stopped
For green. His eyes kept wandering from the road:
He'd see a heron stoic in a bog,
A fold of field, a woods, pronounce them good;
Converse with my mother till his foot forgot
The pressure of progress and the old coupe slowed—

Thirty-five, thirty. . . . We itched, but Father knew
We had all summer to spend beside the point,
Stopped at a slow green light. He's dead now,
And caught between cars on the Interstate, intent
On a strip of macadam laid down like the Law,
So much attention focussed on accident,
How can his children see the things he saw?

Thirty-five

Thirty-five: reaching the outer curve
And turning back, beginning to enclose.
Conserve, an instinct cautions me, conserve:
Water and weed your acre, watch what grows.
The wall around your garden is the price
That must be paid for any paradise.
Another instinct answers that to live
Demands a wall as sensitive as skin —
At sixty let me have a lover's nerve
To let the inside out, the outside in.

The Poet Attempts to Console His Wife, Who Has Just Put His Wallet through the Washing Machine

Don't cry, my love; only my abstract's lost;
My cards, my money, that old photograph
Are mangled to innocent pulp, but I'm still whole.
Love can survive a shattered casserole,
Outlast the water flooding from a bath,
Rise like the phoenix from ashes of burnt toast.
I say it's not your fault. Some Devil's loose
Who's sworn to keep perfection from this house.

Perfection, after all, is just a means —
At least, that's what we said the week we stayed
With that fierce housewife on our honeymoon
Who banished us the whole day from our room
For fear we'd track in mud, or muss the bed.
We laughed and cursed at her five afternoons.
She battled Time with bedspread and with broom,
But we were young, and knew it for our home.

In short, the apple ripens for the taste,
The mint gives up its flavor when it's crushed,
And what the wallet did when it was washed
Was put you in my arms; and so we kissed.

The Infestation

All summer long
big ants have crawled
from our bedroom wall
like dirty words.
We squashed them first
in Kleenex, squirming,
and flushed them down
the toilet; then
when we began
to sense them on
our skin at night,
their feather-feet
more gentle than
our gentlest touch,
we crushed them flat
with books, with shoes,
barefoot, between
index and thumb,
till knotted corpses
glutted the rug
like ace after crumpled
ace of clubs.

Now when we see
an ant appear
and strangely reel
across our floor,
we let him go
in peace to wear
his poison vest,
like the emperor's clothes,
back to the nest,
where the other ants
can lick him clean.
My love, I taste
you in the night,
we twist and turn
and fall asleep,
while death goes on
behind the wall,
at last discreet.

Choirboys and Starlings

for Tim

A few days before you were ten, Tim,
We heard a boys' choir sing Mozart
In the light from a stained-glass window,
The beauty of unbroken voices
As pure as the slate-blue sky
In which, as we drove home that evening,
A sudden grisaille of starlings
Whirled like desires in confusion.

You race time through the mazes
Set into cathedral pavements,
While holding the hands of our guidebooks
We try to unravel the past.
Choirboys turn into starlings.
At ten are you leaving the garden
Where birds bright as flags flute Mozart
To wander a centerless maze?

No. We both know that's nonsense.
At eight and nine I awaited
The coming of ten like salvation,
Like the miraculous instant my feet
Hanging over the edges of chairs
Would at last touch the ground and I'd walk
Straight to a preordained glory.
I wanted to shave and be famous.

Last night you claimed that a hair
Was growing (hooray!) in your armpit.
I grizzle the sink with my shavings
And they whirl down the drain like despair.
Old and young, we're one in our longings
To be something or somewhere we're not.
What birthday wisdom or wishes
Should I offer the maker of maps?

Do you remember in France
Before you could speak the language
How you sat in your classroom and drew,
In colors as deep as your longing,
As pure as the music of Mozart,
A map of the whole U.S.A.?
That map was a map of your heart.
Is *that* the heart of the maze?

If I could play the recorder
As you've tried to teach me, I'd play
In the midst of confusion a tune
That would say what is in me to say.
May all of your wishes come clear, Tim,
Whether or not they come true.
Starlings and choirboys together
Sing love and contentment to you.

For Sarah

you are twelve   you are lovely
still as a stone
in a Japanese garden
never still
you laugh, you cry, you go out
with Amy, with Pam   you come in
you are here   you are there
you are neither here nor there
at night you sleep
I kiss your cheek on the pillow
it is imponderable
you are a grey bird on the beach, a yellow bird
in my maple, moving
behind moving leaves
I cannot fix you
in my glasses, and when I do
I do not recognize you

Balloon Flight

The surprising joy of
Being robbed! After the first shocked
Sense of violation,
Of being so crudely *known,*
And after the bored
Detective had listed our losses,
And we'd gone to the consulate,
And canceled our credit cards,

The sudden recognition, driving north from Barcelona
In our rented car—
Not stolen! A mercy!—
That three hours of looking at the divine
Melancholy of Christ
Crucified in polychrome, of a saint unzipped by the saw,
Of Mary grave with private knowledge,
Were worth more than a thief could imagine wanting.

And then, crossing the border,
Without passport,
Waved on by the indifferent guard,
An elation as of ballast cast off,
As of floating upwards together, free,
Windborne, anonymous,
Nothing left to lose
But each other.

A Fable in Two Languages

I.

L'Oiseau, la Souris, et le Chat

Un petit oiseau chantait
Sous le soleil de mai —
"Qu'il fait beau, qu'il fait beau, fait beau!"
Une souris lui chuchota,
"Ne sais-tu pas que le chat
Cherche par ici, par là,
Un morceau tendre comme toi?
Les petits doivent se taire. C'est la loi!"
L'oiseau chanta encore plus haut —
"Qu'il fait beau, qu'il fait beau, fait beau!"
Un jour vint le chat et mangea
Notre ami l'oiseau. Voilà,
Plus de chansons dans les champs,
On n'entend que le clac-clac des dents.
Et puis le chat prit la souris
Malgré les bons conseils soumis;
Il la mangea, c'est bien dommage,
Bien qu'elle fût silencieuse et sage.
La leçon qu'on apprend — qu'est-ce que c'est?
Qui ne chante jamais, ne chantera jamais.

II.

The Bird, the Mouse, and the Cat

A little bird warbled away,
Gay in the sunlight of May —
"What a day, what a day, day, day!"
"Psst!" hissed a mouse. "Keep it low!
Mister Pussy's out prowling, you know.
He's quite keen of hearing, and oh!
How morsels like you make him drool.
The small must keep still. That's the rule."
The bird sang still louder, "Hooray!
What a day, what a day, day, day!"
One morning, along came the cat
And caught our friend bird. That was that.
A muffled chomp-chomp, and done!
No more songs in the sun.
And next the cat ate — it's not nice —
Despite all its careful advice,
The mouse — popped it into the hopper,
Though so perfectly silent and proper.
The lesson you'll learn, if you're clever?
If you don't ever sing, you won't ever.

Evening Meditation in a Cathedral Town

Transparent on transparency,
A lacewing on the windowpane.
Pale green traceries of vein
In the lancets of its wings sustain
A membrane too fine for the eye.
As tranquil on the mystery
Of glass as if taught by its wings
How to put faith in invisible things,
In slow sweeps back and forth it swings
Its frail antennae thoughtfully,
Like compasses that leave no mark:
Geometers imagining the arc.

In the cathedral treasury
I've gazed, unmoved, at the Virgin's shift,
Draped like dead insect wings—enough,
The histories repeat, to lift
That heap of masonry so high.
Others believed in it; now I
Where the great stained windows raise
Their winged parabolas of praise
Day after day can bring to graze,
Sheepish, my agnostic eye.
Such precious straining of the light
Surprises stone and souls of stone to flight.

Small concentration of the evening air,
Lacewing, I look through you and glass to where
Beyond the fields the late sun condenscends
To denseness, and its true brightness bends
And bursts to beauty where the transparent ends.

Brass Rubbing

We touched the hidden forms
As gently as a lover could,
Then took the wax and rubbed
Until a knight and lady stood
Revealed, like breath on glass;
And now, benign and timeless, they
Are watching from a frame
The mingled pressures of our lives:
What we, when rubbed, become.

Biographical Notes

Charles W. Pratt, a graduate of Princeton, has taught secondary school English for twenty-seven years, for the last nineteen years of that period at Phillips Exeter Academy. He received a Diploma in English Studies from Cambridge University and has also done graduate work at the Bread Loaf School of English at Middlebury College.

He, his wife Joan, their daughter Sarah and son Tim live in Brentwood, New Hampshire, on a small apple orchard.

:><::><::><:

Arthur Balderacchi, a member of the faculty in the Department of the Arts at the University of New Hampshire, teaches drawing there. He is a graduate of Duke University and the University of Georgia and is a former chair of the Department of the Arts. His work is in a number of private collections.

:><::><::><:

This
second
printing of
six hundred copies
is printed photo-offset
from the original letterpress;
on Mohawk Superfine Text in a
typeface called Caledonia by
The Anthoensen Press.
The drawings have
been reproduced
photo-offset.

⋈⋈⋈⋈⋈⋈

⋈⋈⋈

⋈⋈